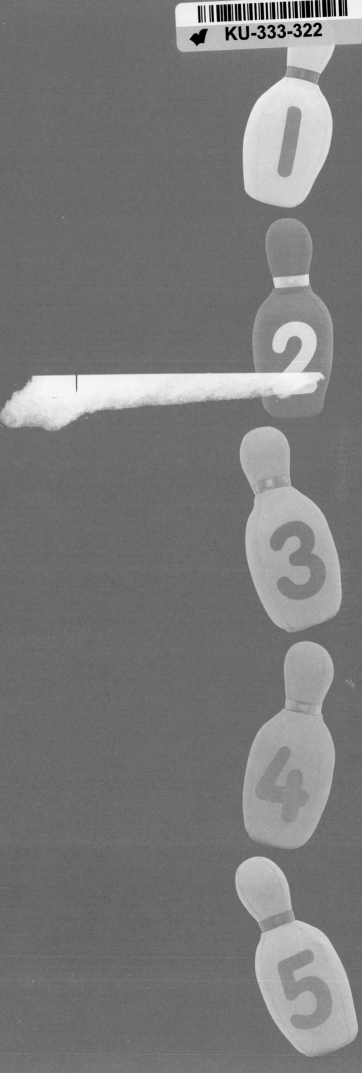

J. 510

323190

early learner

Playing with numbers

This book belongs to

_____

Joanna Babb BSc PGCE MSc

LORENZ BOOKS

Joanna Babb is a primary schoolteacher in London with a special interest in numeracy and information technology. She studied psychology at the University of Birmingham and has an MSc in Cognitive Development and a PGCE from the University of Cambridge. Joanna has worked for an educational publisher developing courses in maths for primary schoolchildren.

contents

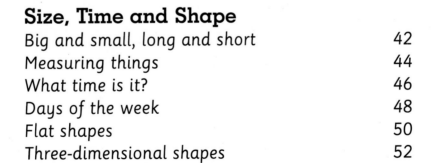

Learning Together

This book is divided into four topics: counting and recognizing numbers; addition and subtraction; size, time and shapes; and patterns and groups. These chapters reflect the National Numeracy Strategy for Reception and Year 1 and the Early Learning goals for the Foundation Stage. Some activities are more difficult than others, and you will need to assess your own child and focus on relevant activities. So, for example, if they are finding it difficult to count 10 objects, avoid moving them on to the next activity, counting to 20, until they have mastered the previous concept. Although the book can be dipped into, most children will find it easier to start with counting before they move on to other concepts. When a child has mastered a concept, they can tick this off on their progress chart at the back of the book – but you should remember to continue to revise the mastered concept, so that it isn't forgotten.

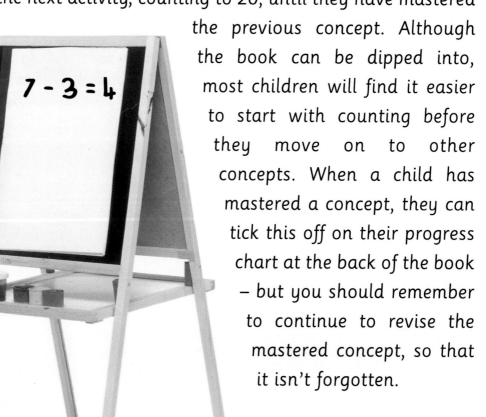

Recording maths

In the early years at school, the emphasis is on practical maths. Writing numbers and recording sums is important, but not until a child really understands what the numbers mean. Only ask your child to write the numbers or answers when you feel they understand, for example, that the symbol '3' means three things.

Working with your child

Find a quiet, cosy place to look at the book together without any interruptions. Spend a short time, perhaps 5–10 minutes, looking at the book, and if the child wants to stop then let them. Learning should be seen as fun. Children are naturally curious and keen to find out more, but pushing them may put them off learning.

Other things to do with your child

Practical maths using real-life situations is the best maths you can do with your child. You can do maths with everyday things in your home. Try involving your child when you hang out the washing. Put coloured pegs into repeating patterns, for example. Count the socks or add the socks and shirts together.

Children's learning

Everyone learns at a different rate, and often a child can do things we consider difficult, but can't do other things we think of as easy. The main thing is to encourage your child to see maths as a fun thing to do.

In this chapter, you will learn to count to 10, then to 20, and then finally to 100. You will also start to count in 2s and find out about odd and even numbers. As well as learning to count, you will learn what 'more' and 'less' mean, how to order numbers and how to estimate amounts.

counting and numbers

Can you count to 10?

Molly has organized a birthday party for her teddy bears. Each teddy has a balloon showing his age. Can you join each teddy to the cake that shows the right number of candles for his age? The first one has been done for you.

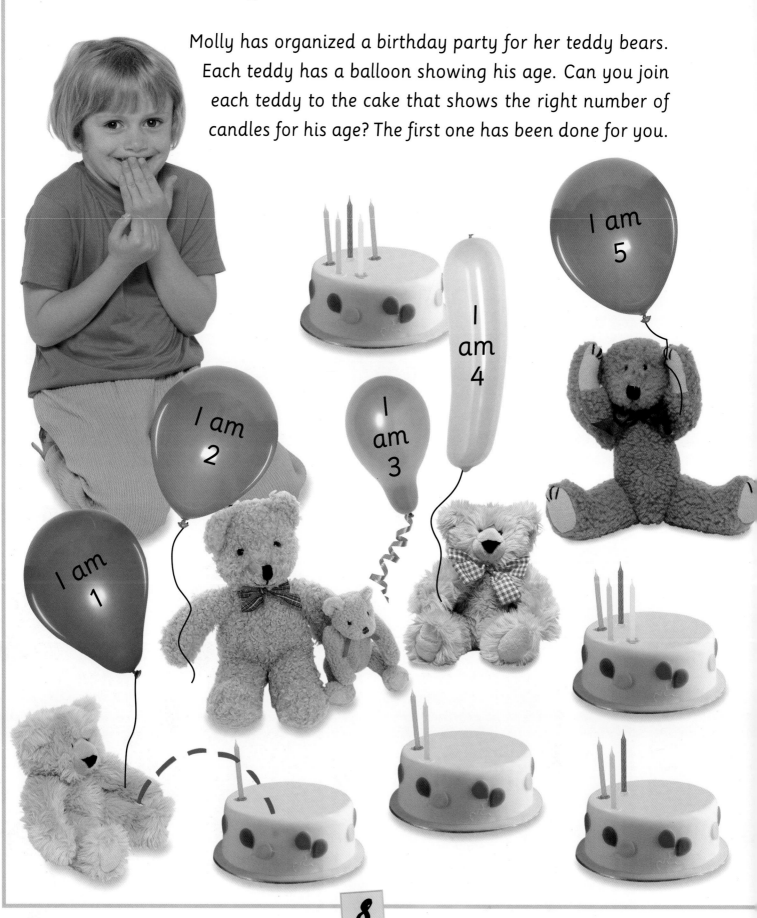

I am 6

I am 9

I am 10

I am 7

I am 8

1 one

2 two

3 three

4 four

5 five

6 six

7 seven

8 eight

9 nine

10 ten

Now try this!

Write over the numbers below. Make a birthday badge and write your age on it.

1 2 3 4 5
6 7 8 9 10

Counting from 11 to 20

Ben is playing in the garden. Can you count how many things there are around him?

11
12
13
14
15
16
17
18
19
20

12
apples

14
clouds

13
leaves

11
ants

10

16 ladybirds

19 butterflies

17 bees

15 sunflowers

20 pebbles

18 snails

Now try this!

Can you write the numbers from 11 to 20?

11 12 13 14
15 16 17 18
19 20

All the way to 100

A hungry monkey has taken some of the numbered fruits from the tree. You will find the fruits on the grass at the foot of the tree. Can you draw the missing apple in the right place on the tree and colour it in? Then write the correct number on it. Now draw all the other missing fruits on the tree and write the numbers on the fruits.

Now try this!

Count from 1 to 100, pointing at each number as you say it aloud. Can you count in 10s? Write over the numbers below.

10 20 30 40
50 60 70 80
90 100

2

96

78

53

1		3	4	5	6	7	8	9	10
11	12	13		15	16	17	18	19	20
21	22	23	24	25	26	27	28	29	
31	32	33	34	35	36	37	38	39	40
41	42	43	44	45	46	47	48	49	50
51	52		54	55	56	57	58	59	60
61	62	63	64	65		67	68	69	70
71	72	73	74	75	76	77		79	80
81	82	83	84		86	87	88	89	90
91	92	93	94	95		97	98	99	100

85

14

66

30

Can you count in 2s?

Jenny and Rebecca are helping the animals
go into the ark to escape from the rain.
Start with the tigers and help the girls
count the animals as they go in in 2s.
Write over the numbers
underneath the animals.
Can you fill in the
missing numbers on
the flags?

Now try this!

Find some things that come in 2s. Look out for 2 wheels on a bike, 2 boots and other 2s.

15

Odds and evens

Peter needs to give a ball to each of his players. Write in the odd numbers on the balls and join each player to the ball with the same number of dots. Using a different-coloured pen, do the same for the even-numbered players on the next page.

'odd' socks

Now try this!

Help the odd team by writing over the numbers on their shirts.

1 3 5 7 9

Now count to check you know all the odd numbers.

4

2

8

10

6

2

4

6

8

10

'even' socks

Who has more, who has less?

There are lots of cats, teddies and books on this page. Count them and work out who has more and who has less.

Peter has 5 cats and Lucy has 1 cat.
Who has more cats?

Who has less soft toys?

Now try this!

Count how many soft toys you have in your bedroom. Count how many books there are. Are there more toys? Which is less?

Who has less books?

Which scooter has more teddies?

Ordering numbers

Suzy needs to follow the stepping stones in
the right order so that she can get home.
Can you help her by pointing to the stones
she needs to step on?

Now try this!

Write these numbers
in the right order.

4   2   9   1   3

6   10   5   8   7

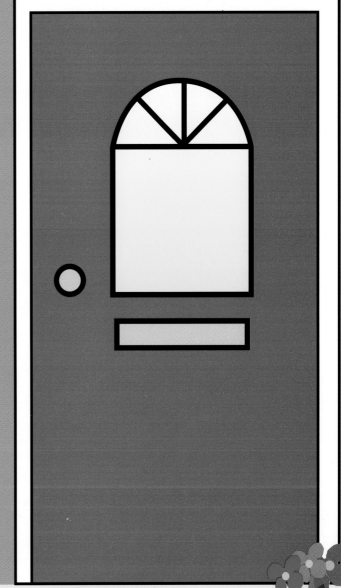

Estimating amounts

Matthew the magician has lots of things to use in his magic shows. Can you guess how many of each item he has? Hold the book against a mirror to see if you are right.

6 juggling balls

6 flowers

9 magic wands

5 rabbits

7 top hats

5 scarves

10 teddies

4 wizard hats

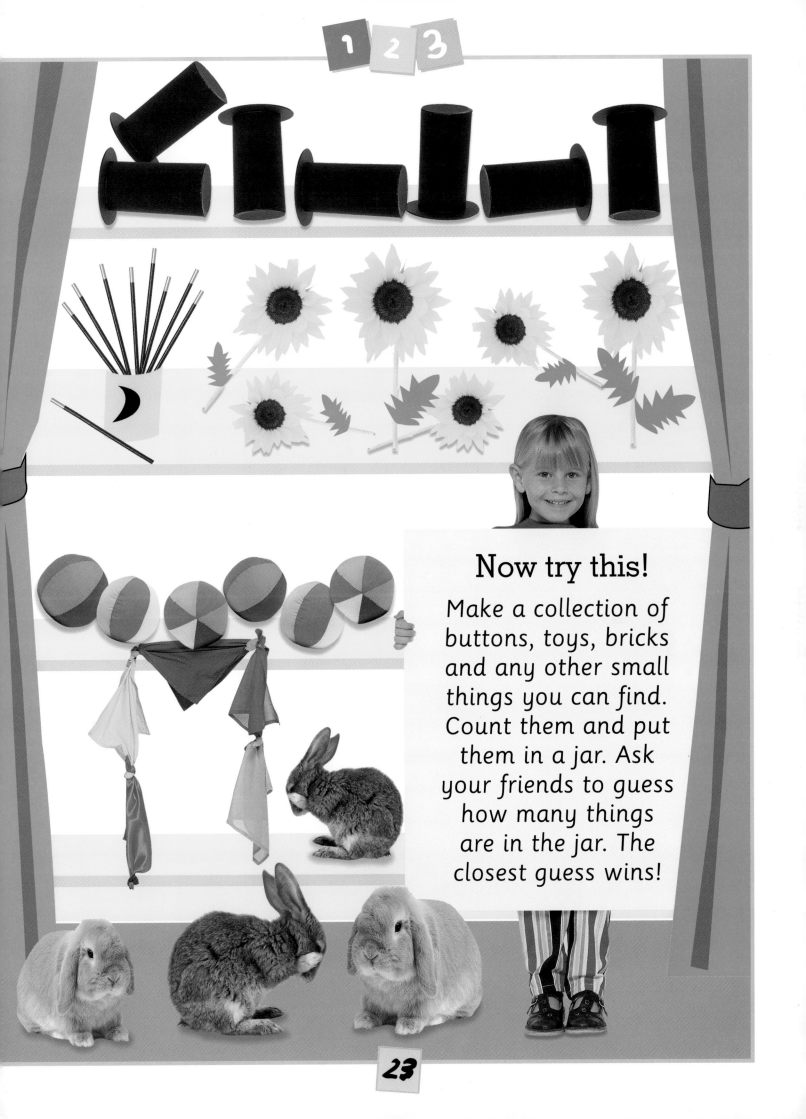

Now try this!

Make a collection of buttons, toys, bricks and any other small things you can find. Count them and put them in a jar. Ask your friends to guess how many things are in the jar. The closest guess wins!

This chapter teaches you how to add and how to subtract. It shows you how to add by combining groups of objects and how to subtract by taking objects away from a group. You will also find out how to double numbers up, and learn the numbers that add together to make 5 and 10.

Adding and subtracting

More and less

Sam wants to be a builder. He can add more windows to these houses. Or he can take windows away so that they have less.

Draw 1 more window. How many now? ☐

Cross out 2 windows to make 2 less. How many now? ☐

Draw 1 more window. How many now? ☐

Now try this!

What number is 1 more than ...?

2 ☐ 3 ☐ 4 ☐

What number is 1 less than ...?

7 ☐ 8 ☐ 9 ☐

Draw 2 more windows. How many now? ☐

Cross out 1 window to make 1 less. How many now? ☐

Make the total

Peter has just finished hanging up the washing. Can you count the different things on each washing line and write down how many items there are altogether?

3 + 2 = ☐

2 + 4 = ☐

4 + 3 = ☐

Jasmine has grown some pretty flowers. Can you help her by finding the two bunches of flowers that add up to make the number on each vase?

Now try this!

Can you do these sums?

1 + 4 = ☐

5 + 5 = ☐

3 + 5 = ☐

4 + 1 = ☐

Use your fingers to help you add.

Counting on and counting back

Can you help Pirate Penny and Pirate Pete reach the treasure?
Play this game with a partner. You will need a dice
and two counters. Roll the dice and count on that
number of stepping stones. The winner is the first one
to reach the treasure.

11

10

9

3

1

2

4

17

18

12

16

19

20

13

15

8

14

7

Now try this!
Play the game counting back from the treasure to the beginning. Place your counters on 20. Roll the dice and the first pirate back to the island is the winner.

6

5

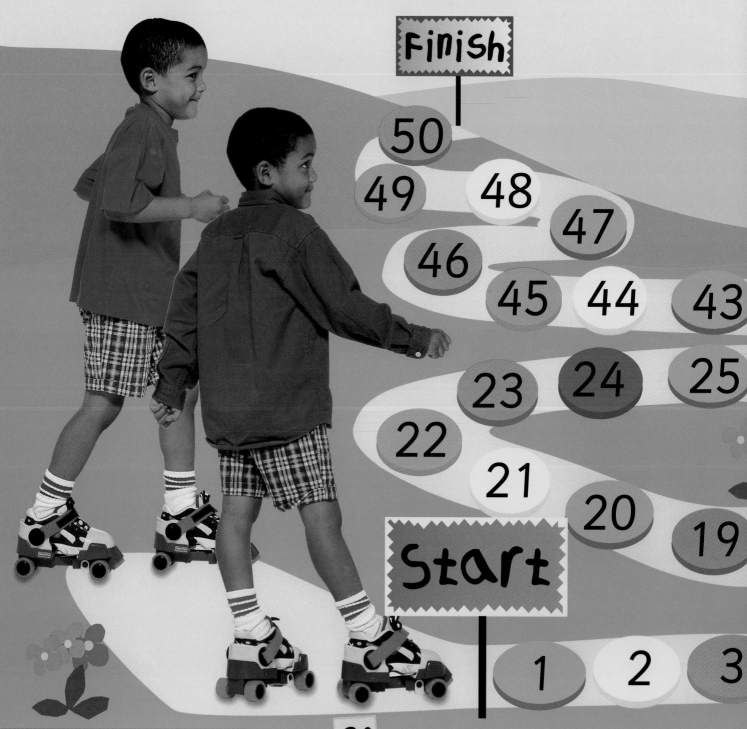

Doubling numbers

Alex and Andrew love racing each other around the park. Play this game with a partner. You will need a dice and two counters. Roll the dice and count the spots. Double the number of spots and move your counter by that amount. Who will win the race?

Finish

50

49 48

47

46

45 44 43

23 24 25

22

21

20

19

Start

1 2 3

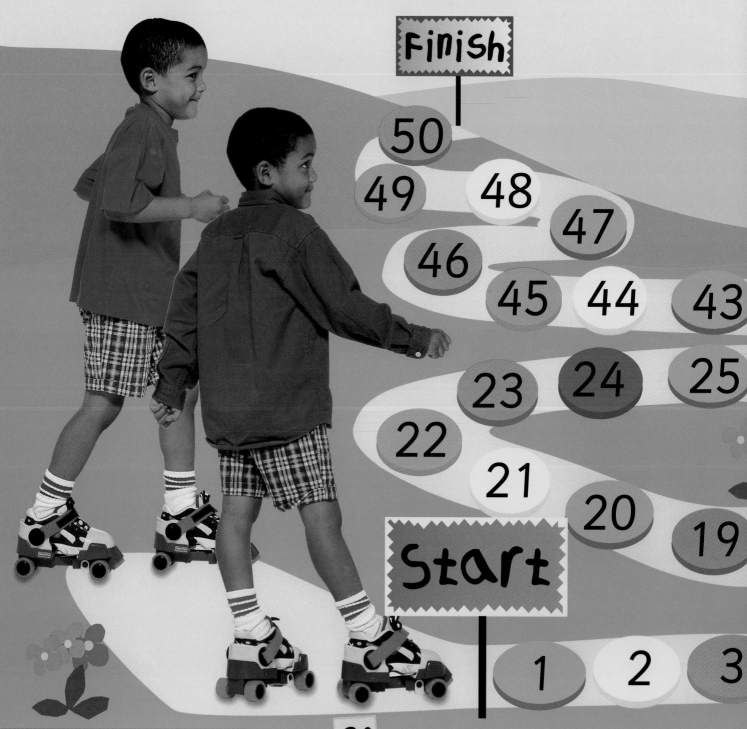

Now try this!

Can you write the doubles for these numbers?

$1 + 1 =$ ☐ $4 + 4 =$ ☐

$2 + 2 =$ ☐ $5 + 5 =$ ☐

$3 + 3 =$ ☐ $6 + 6 =$ ☐

37 36 35

38 34

39

40 33

42 41

26 27 28 29 30 31 32

15 14 13

16 12

17

18 11

10

4 5 6 7 8 9

Taking away

Play this game with a partner. You will need a dice and 30 buttons or counters. Each player has 15 toys to put away. Roll the dice and take away that number of toys from your page by covering them with some of your counters. The first person who puts away all their toys wins.

Now try this!

Take away and write the answers in the boxes.

2 - 2 = ☐   7 - 2 = ☐

3 - 2 = ☐   8 - 2 = ☐

4 - 2 = ☐   9 - 2 = ☐

5 - 2 = ☐   10 - 2 = ☐

6 - 2 = ☐

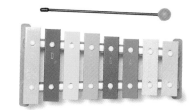

How many more do you need?

These children are in the playground. How many more hoops are needed so that all the children in the group have one?

There are 7 children. 3 children have hoops. How many more hoops do you need so all the children have a hoop?

How many more tricycles do you need so they all have one?

Now try this!

Write the missing numbers in the boxes.

$2 + \boxed{} = 4$ $5 + \boxed{} = 7$

$3 + \boxed{} = 5$ $6 + \boxed{} = 8$

$4 + \boxed{} = 6$

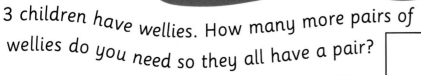

3 children have wellies. How many more pairs of wellies do you need so they all have a pair?

Making 10

This vet is very busy. Count the animals with each child and write the number in the box. Join the pairs of children whose pets added together make a total of 10 animals.

Vet

Now try this!

Write the missing numbers in the boxes.

1 + ☐ = 10   4 + ☐ = 10

☐ + 8 = 10   ☐ + 5 = 10

3 + ☐ = 10   6 + ☐ = 10

This chapter shows you how to describe and compare objects of different sizes, and how to measure them. You will learn about flat shapes and three-dimensional shapes, such as cubes and cylinders. You will begin to tell the time on a clock and learn the names of the days of the week.

Size, Time and Shape

Big and small, long and short

Michael has a big teddy and a small teddy. Can you join each bear to its clothes? Which belong to the big teddy and which to the small teddy?

Who is the shortest and who is the tallest? Number these pictures from 1 to 4, starting with the shortest person first.

Now try this!

Find 10 toys and count them. How tall are they? Place them in a line in order of their size. Put the tallest toy first and the shortest toy last.

Measuring things

Jack and Susie are in their playroom measuring some things. Can you measure each object by counting the items they have used for measuring? Write each number in the box.

How many teddies tall is this chest of drawers?

How many balls long is this train?

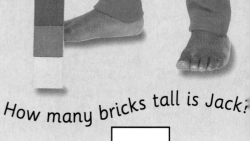

How many bricks tall is Jack?

Now try this!

Measure different things in your room using items like buttons, straws and building blocks. How many building bricks tall is your bed? Find out how many teddies tall you are.

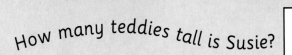

How many teddies tall is Susie?

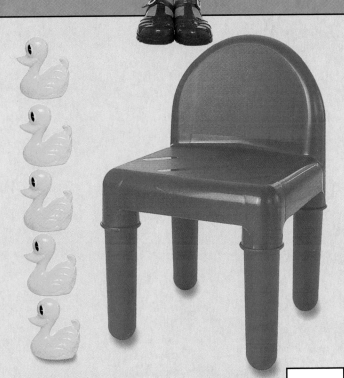

How many ducks high is this chair?

What time is it?

We do things at different times of the day. Look at the clocks and work out which is the right order starting from the beginning of the day. Number the pictures from 1 to 7 starting with the first one.

7 o'clock.
It's time to get up.

8 o'clock.
It's breakfast time.

3 o'clock.
It's time to go home.

12 o'clock.
It's lunchtime.

9 o'clock.
School starts.

Now try this!

Make some drawings of yourself doing things at different times of the day. Put them all in the right order. Find out what time you get up and what time you go to bed.

6 o'clock.
It's dinner time.

8 o'clock.
It's bedtime.

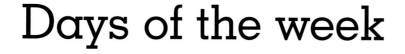

Days of the week

Do you know the days of the week?
Clap each day in turn as you say
them out loud. Look at the pictures of
these children enjoying different activities.
On which day of the week would you like to do
each of these things? Draw lines to join each
activity to a day of the week.

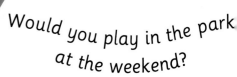

Would you play in the park
at the weekend?

When would you go swimming?

Which day would you like to
go skateboarding?

Monday

Tuesday

Wednesday

Thursday

Friday

Now try this!

Make a chart with the 7 days of the week. Draw a picture of what you would like to do each day.

When do you want to skate?

When would you like to skip?

Which day would you like to paint?

Which day would you go fishing?

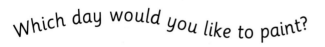

Saturday

Sunday

Flat shapes

Chris, Sam, George and Toby all live in Shape Street. Can you find the right-shaped home for each one?

How many rectangular windows are there on this house?

There are 3 round windows on this house. Can you add 3 more? How many are there now?

circle

square

How many triangular windows can you count?

There are 5 big square windows on the house and 2 small windows on the door. How many windows are there in total?

rectangle

triangle

Now try this!
How many sides do these shapes have?

square

circle

triangle

rectangle

Three-dimensional shapes

These children are having fun at a party. How many three-dimensional shapes can you see? Count them and write the total for each shape in the boxes at the bottom of the page.

This is a cone.

This is a cube. Each side is exactly the same size.

This flat box shape is a cuboid.

Now try this!

Look in your bedroom. Find toys that are shaped like a sphere or a cube or a cuboid. How many shapes can you find?

This round shape is called a sphere.

This shape is a cylinder.

This three-dimensional triangle is called a pyramid.

This chapter shows you how to see and make patterns. You will learn how to match things and sort things into groups. It shows you how to make a simple graph, which is a good way of displaying information easily.

Patterns and Groups

Finding patterns

Look at the patterns made by these pictures. Do you see how the pattern goes all the way along the line? Say the names of the objects in each pattern, for example cone, cube, cone, cube. Then clap the pattern. Clap your hands together, clap your knees, clap your hands, clap your knees. For a pattern like sock, sock, glove, you can clap hands, hands, knees, hands, hands, knees.

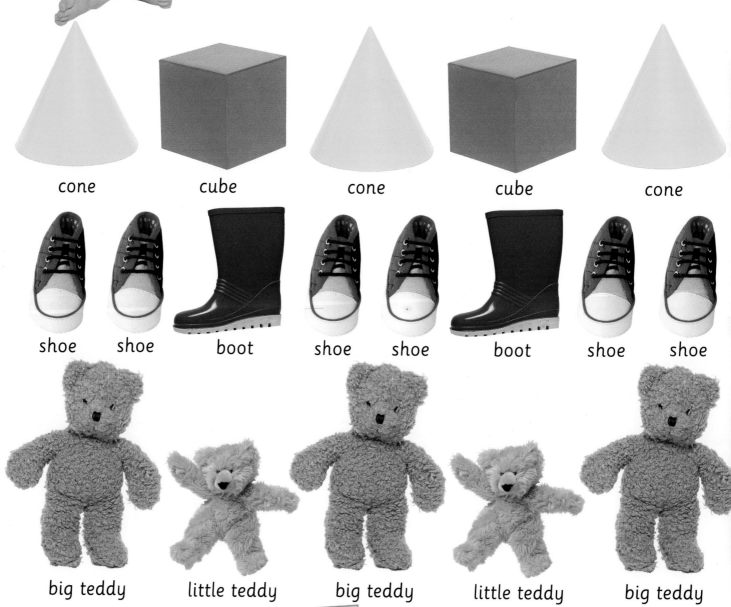

| cone | cube | cone | cube | cone |

| shoe | shoe | boot | shoe | shoe | boot | shoe | shoe |

| big teddy | little teddy | big teddy | little teddy | big teddy |

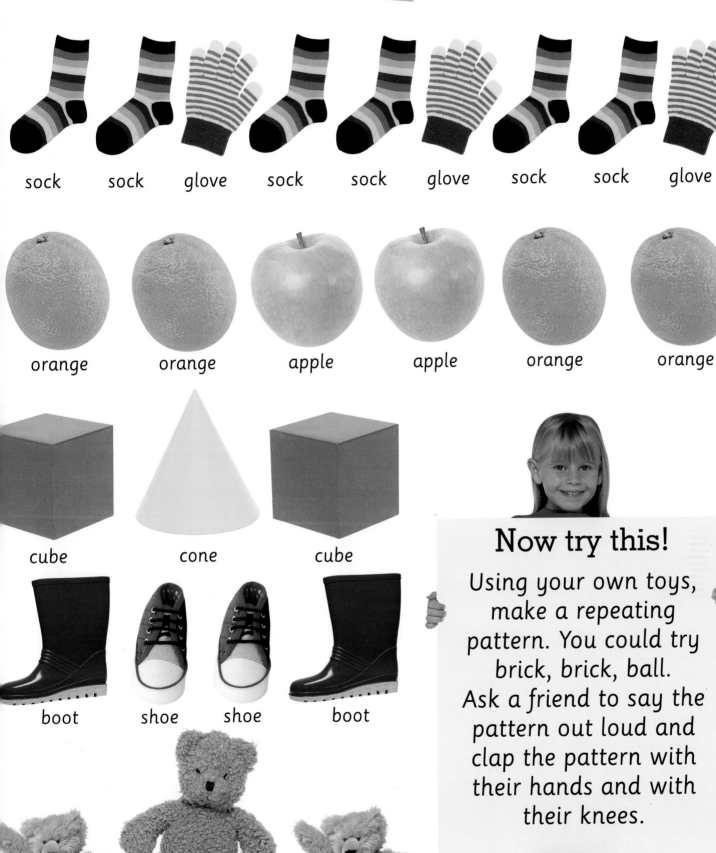

sock   sock   glove   sock   sock   glove   sock   sock   glove

orange   orange   apple   apple   orange   orange

cube   cone   cube

boot   shoe   shoe   boot

little teddy   big teddy   little teddy

Now try this!

Using your own toys, make a repeating pattern. You could try brick, brick, ball. Ask a friend to say the pattern out loud and clap the pattern with their hands and with their knees.

Sorting and matching

Lucy has lots of pets. Can you sort them into groups by drawing a line around the ones that match?

Now try this!

Collect some building bricks or find some leaves in the garden. Look for bricks that are different colours or for leaves that are different shapes. Ask an adult if it is safe to pick the leaves. Then sort the bricks or the leaves into your own groups.

Reading graphs

Neil likes playing badminton. The pictogram or picture graph opposite shows how many children in Neil's class like 4 different sports. Graphs are a way of showing information without writing it all out in words.

Look at the pictogram carefully. The sports activities are listed down the left hand side of the pictogram. The numbers appear across the bottom of the pictogram. You can help Neil answer the questions below.

How many children like cycling?

How many like skateboarding?

How many like ball games?

How many like swimming?

What is the most popular sport?

What is the least popular sport?

Now try this!

Which sport do you like best? Draw a picture of yourself on the pictogram to show which sport you like best. Now add drawings to show your friends' favourite sports.

Skateboarding

Ball Games

Swimming

Cycling

Sports / Numbers

	1	2	3	4

61

Progress Chart

Record your progress here.
Place a tick in the box when you have completed each section.

When you have completed a chapter, fill out the certificate.

Counting and Numbers

Adding and Subtracting

Size, Time and Shape

Patterns and Groups

certificate of achievement

Counting and Numbers

yess

is a brilliant
EARLY LEARNER!

certificate of achievement

Size, Time and Shape

Gess

is a brilliant
EARLY LEARNER!

certificate of achievement

Adding and Subtracting

syoss

is a brilliant
EARLY LEARNER!

certificate of achievement

Patterns and Groups

yess

is a brilliant
EARLY LEARNER!

This edition is published by Lorenz Books

Lorenz Books is an imprint of Anness Publishing Ltd
Hermes House, 88–89 Blackfriars Road
London SE1 8HA
tel. 020 7401 2077; fax 020 7633 9499
www.lorenzbooks.com; info@anness.com

Published in the USA by Lorenz Books,
Anness Publishing Inc., 27 West 20th Street
New York, NY 10011; fax 212 807 6813

This edition distributed in Australia by
Pan Macmillan Australia
Level 18, St Martins Tower, 31 Market St, Sydney,
NSW 2000; tel. 1300 135 113; fax 1300 135 103;
email customer.service@macmillan.com.au

This edition distributed in the UK by Aurum Press Ltd
25 Bedford Avenue, London WC1B 3AT
tel. 020 7637 3225; fax 020 7580 2469

This edition distributed in the USA by National Book
Network, 4720 Boston Way, Lanham, MD 20706
tel. 301 459 3366; fax 301 459 1705
www.nbnbooks.com

This edition distributed in Canada by
General Publishing, 895 Don Mills Road
400–402 Park Centre, Toronto, Ontario M3C 1W3
tel. 416 445 3333; fax 416 445 5991
www.genpub.com

This edition distributed in New Zealand by
David Bateman Ltd, 30 Tarndale Grove
Off Bush Road, Albany, Auckland
tel. (09) 415 7664; fax (09) 415 8892

A CIP catalogue record for this book is available
from the British Library.

Publisher: Joanna Lorenz
Managing Editor: Linda Fraser
Editors: Joy Wotton and Molly Perham
Design: Alix Wood of Applecart
Photography: Jane Burton, John Daniels,
  John Freeman, Robert Pickett, Kim Taylor
  and Lucy Tizard

The publishers would like to thank all the children
who appear in this book.

10 9 8 7 6 5 4 3 2 1